J.
MICHAEL
YATES

THE QUALICUM PHYSICS

THE KANCHENJUNGA PRESS
San Francisco and Vancouver
1975

Published simultaneously in Canada and the United States by the Kanchenjunga Press, San Francisco and Vancouver. Orders and inquiries: In Canada: c/o The Sono Nis Press, 4565 Church Street, Delta, British Columbia V4K 2K9; In the U.S.A.: The Kanchenjunga Press, 22 Rio Vista Lane, Red Bluff, California 96080.

Typography by George Payerle.

This work has been broadcast by CBC Radio.

Let there be no man who is best among us.
If there exists such a one, let him
Be it elsewhere. And among others.

— Herakleitos

MANTÍLI

In the Kalamatianós, *one dancer separates himself from, or joins himself to the others by a* mantíli, *a kerchief or table napkin.*

The other participants contiguate by hand, unlike the separate one who is of them only by virtue of something artificial, unmetabolic, of a different modality of time — without blood, utterly.

The séparatiste *may invent as he will within the circle; the others — without the apparent freedom afforded him by his linen hinge — cannot possibly hope to mime the configurations of his steps and gestures, if to do so is desirable. Among them they attempt to effect a motile harmonium of their linked mortalities.*

Separated by mantíli *is the leader, magnificent in the whirling mobile of his inventions, while the rest, restricted as they are by their less flexible relationships, follow along and find a certain satiety in their awkward unison.*

Separated by mantíli *is the least of the dancers: not at all the leader, but the single follower, permitted to dance only for ornamental reasons. Although he appears at the fore of the moving and nearly closed circle, he must exert far more energy in his rhapsodic gyrations. One senses that, should his stamina give, the rest might overtake and possibly trample him beneath their vaster inertia and gravity.*

Perhaps he invents with such energy and imagination only to keep himself company in his isolation from the rest.

Whether the dance might proceed without either element (whoever follows, whoever leads) is a cycloid and constant deliberation.

Time of the dance changes, time of the clock passes, circumference of the circle lessens. All circle separate but together and joined to the almost nascent dancer by a mere metaphor.

This is a very ancient music; its name in imprecise translation: I AM THE ONE DANCE AND I GO ON STILL.

For Hatch
From the one who squandered a lifetime
Failing perfectly to explain away
The destructions.

And ai *it was a wormish wisdom:*
Overripeness overcoming the everything,

Rhapsode of animal and ornament
In quest of place to assignate,

One neither an odd nor even number,
Concealed in the green globe, a numb pith of rot

Alive far out on the limbo twig,
Σοφία, ὀρθοί: *so spake the lime snake,*

For every coil a recoil, a hope it was,
Let there be let be, and it was not so.

Now it has me, now I have it:
The viper is in the snake, the bite,

The utterance, or the ear; the rich round
Clarities beneath the moving darkness of the shells,

Border between garden and jungle
Bansheeing into the great unclear.

The short dream is electric, essentially,
An angel of arc between coeval poles.

No, not exactly an sich, en soi,
Only how to bloody work it;

What anode, what cathode shorted sich
To load the epode circuit?

Strewing seed I passed this way,
In one hand or another the fecund tree,

Never a thought my traces might be followed
And the Vishnu/Siva apple fall to me.

How to exact the figure from the stone
Without gravel by the throatful,

Hands running blood and hypertactile,
Lungs of the thought in collapse

Of the quotidian silicosis, ages
Of my angel so infinitesimal

No word of time arrives to express them;
Eons flow into figure like dawn birds

Crossing a drunken window. Pages
Of law are not for sale. Sing,

Stupefy who will hear, sing them.
The pages exist purely for the sake of gifting.

Inquire never: cost of the binding.
Sunset upon the interrogative peaks

And still two eagles divided by seven
Dalmatians does not equal the edge

Of a single Zeitwort; Vanitas
Vanitatum *said all there'd ever be,*

All else being vanity; the fourteen stations
Of the sad metric which appears

Like an angry unfamiliar cur
At a little-used lateral door

Are not located atop fourteen
Worn hills of equal height.

Command the Sufi to sing the one
Called "Sophie Never Sang."

May I help you?
I should like to die. And rare, s.v.p.

Suffer the risen demon. Once sat I
At Lucifer's left hand.

Achtung! Wisdom, ye orthodox,
Wisdom! The Word.

The word, in the beginning, was maybe.
Outside the beginning, it was felt somewhat fleshy.

One then thought: why not substitute beginning?
In experiment the regressus was declared confusing.

Required still was another beginning —
Hopefully, one without ending. And another word.

It grew progressively more difficult
To distinguish the beginning from the beginning.

In the beginning, among other souvenirs, the word.
Several grooves comprehended the shape, silence.

Never was it admitted aloud, for fear that to do so
Would be to separate word from what it advocates.

In the word the beginning began.
Also within the beginning was the law,

And two stone tablets wrestled the mountain down
In evidence the summit had been acquired.

The rocks were at rest throughout the beginning
Before the hewing of forms began. And the chiselling.

When, finally, word was made sound,
It was at once born and, in mid-spine, broken.

It was first employed in august command
To one engaging in something noisy . . .

As if the attention of someone or something were necessary . . .
As if there might be no beginning whatsoever otherwise . . .

All night the warring of the water against my edge of stone.
Never invoke nature for terror it might once hear you

Above the wind, a hellborn rain, and stones against all stones.
At birth your presence passed perfectly into note.

The salt so stronger in the older oceans, near the older lands,
More has died there. Parts intensify the sea.

From the younger ranges, here, too much fresh water
Dilutes the bits strung once together into breath.

Pyrrhic fagotti *flame once*-concerti
Toward the sum where the pyrotechnician,

Estremo, effimero, *oxidizes alive*
While the oxen peep their piccolos.

The Spitzklicker *metaphysical yo-yos*
I follow in and again in — Io, ἐγώ,

This uneverlasting vida entre sueños,
Wind in the woods losing gain

Ab initio, *concupiscence the sole property of the abject,*
Inalienable figleaves in the pursuit of Freude,

Even in the green and verbal solstice,
Unsummoned interstices of soul,

All the good beasts going down without teeth,
A delicate crevasse, the cool coulisse,

Hale empty beneath soft shadow-sky
Burnt blind by sudden and uninvited light.

Voice of the oboe, which sounds all
One definitely does not wish to know, ordered

The mountain man wear down to the sea.
More of wave than angle, now, he descended,

Intook as many fathoms as he could,
Then noted aloud: *That fills* fast *all of me.*

We're learning, and, soon now, it will begin:
The salinity which fashions into pillar, word, and skin.

I become more buoyant, if not less wet. Art. Art —
Gaudiest of colourations on the killer silhouette.

The ghost delivers. Somewhere: a trigger depresses.
The chambered naught chambers not in metaphor, but wars;

Stakes of riot driven midden into midden
To triangulate still another falling form.

A man was no damned thing at all.
Motion or so on a compass face.

A few turns of a dial's close watch.
Gauzy remembrance of a race.

A bit of tissue blowing down a beach: said intelligent,
Supposed delicate, known imperfect, most degradable. . . .

Ashes to ashes and dust to dust. When water is almost all of us?
What small mineral we are strewn across the distance of darkness

Between stars. The coloured spectacles of language
Unsyzygize phases of the word for word.

Some lie and call it truth and believe it.
Some lie and give it the lie and believe it.

I was born almost neverywhere, yesternow; learned, forgot,
Lied, and died — precisely same time, same place.

Within the chambered naught moves
The mirror-maze called belief:

Each grotesquerie a dead-head,
A still uncharted reef.

Waltz of the future between scalpel and suture,
Estuarial ennui . . . delivery of death to death . . .

The living stand and watch the stream,
These soft collisions, this oldest wrath.

No violence at all, this;
The interspersion is a roil of ease;

To see it, to become it well,
Stay very still and do not breathe.

Moon the hunger, lighthouse the barter, sound
Of surf not a blue excuse nor simply wizening reason

To sequester more westerly in this westering season.
Vox populi dies in the pebble larynx of the tide.

It is not the death but the death before
Which bevels the good chartreuse with orange.

The mindlessness of mindless things draws mind.
One dim of dawn: the doomed beak divides: the dumb bird sings

Like a string of a primitive instrument tuned
Beyond beauty toward breaking, toward the codic ping.

The movement itself is mindless
Between the that and this of way.

Blue, one after another blue grotto of day.
The gymnosophy: Never is it too late to fail.

Into form I insert myself and become one word. Why not all.
Once I mistook me for the world and had to subtract my life.

Hurricane's weathervane, the weathervane in the tornado,
Tornado's weathervane; hurry, Cain, Cain, hurry;

At the red line, the blood line will cleave the wad
Into hemispheres, other spheres, other fears,

And the fear which circles full. The present ice-age
Begins in the eyes of a youth in Fairbanks or in Thule.

Bits of a world seem never quite the same
Rising as they did going down.

The retina of my right ear keeps a closed watch on the auditory landscape.
Jagged ozone and old testament clouds on the south horizon of a vowel.

Beware the body wearing the cloak of openness.
In any language only the word indifferent is substantial.

The ordering principle of memory is decay, one more
Muniment against hot light to pry.

Let go now while the letting's good;
Let it slide, let it drift, let it flow away.

The waves break and break and break
Against the coastlands of the ear —

Decreation of the moment first, then the hour, day,
A month supplanted by a gone, and finally the year.

Because I had never glimpsed the high cairns at the borders
Of possibility, I worked the impossible repeatedly.

Comfort isn't given to the hand of probability.
Be satisfied to seek a hollow tree.

You will forget this secret of your now and here:
You are paying in full a debt you didn't incur.

The immensities between land and land commanded
The tides in the solitary cells of my body to come.

Your reinforced bridges over innocuous perils,
My weakening spans above dangers most ominous because dreamed,

I have come not to close questions, but discharge them;
Nor to dispel enigmas, but to charge them;

To give fang and sting to this bush of garden snakes,
To invenomate your pale guardians of the usual,

To wait solitary thirty-seven years on round death row;
Time will tell. I'll listen. There won't be time, I'll never know.

Acknowledge my demand for deep mandolin: When
I translate I become another maker's skin.

You were the fire-lined fornix I passed through into the dark,
And I, merely another green helix dervishing by.

Winterset of the wombat and the patience of the dingos
About the firelight border is boundless.

Mountains, in distance looking monticule, are perhaps the bait
Allures in members of a rocky beach from depth unforeseen —

Figures awesome, altitudinous, vulnerable beyond
Short sight, and too intolerably exceeding reach.

I have spoken before from beneath the sea.
Two orbesque stones clapped together subsurface;

Therefore you did not hear me. Gather
The feathers as they fall; they won't help you to fly.

Arrange them one way, another, still another,
And reason: you did not see what lost them die.

I would cause labyrinth from the alveolus, solarize the child,
And resculpt the great continents of superstition.

You and I are the anti-particulars.
The indrawn gust blows us away.

The blast I almost irresist inhales
Me to the sacs of unfurious lungs.

For cause too covert for me, it clings,
The three-ring masque of sanity.

Unnoticed in their very midst, I in my booth of flames,
Coloured bird prohibited coloured cage

By behemoth numb absents the dreamed-of rage.
At the closing of the bud, the perfect solvent

Will rain, cosmetic sills streak away, and through
The glaucomic pane: an unwarned lighthouse

On a rock in atrophy, beam dimming, maniacally whirling
A hoarse, black-lensed warning, mechanics without feeling,

And it will be time: the hour of no space at hand:
It will be time.

Each morning I took up my body like a dependable axe
And went forth to unbraid green from green. After opening each

Misty envelope, and twilight gave us home again,
I replaced it in its corner until once more required.

Wind of ice, water of fire,
Damned are the eyes of the man who lives

To see the swamps of a life solidify
And all his substantial traces go to mire.

Thermal currents circle me higher in my preterity,
Too late for substantial shore, too early for the sea.

When the surf salt crusting your lips becomes,
At last, without question, the taste of your taste,

It will be uncertainly too late to remark
All things have always been in motion,

And all things mobile have always been at rest.
Rock — only — is the wearing, as in

Wearing of water against water,
Of wind against wind. Your impertinent

Terrorettes to the melodious alone;
Listen with conscientience to the warfare of your stones.

I too insisted through the valley of the broken names
Where traps escape the inhabitants they tame,

Yow, but the numbers in quest of cage are unknown
And presumed infinite. Inside their fugitive disguises,

The huge enclosures dream huge emptiness, emptiness, while tiny lives
Inside them blink undetected and move within slowly scudding umbra.

All light long the humans observe the humans.
Tonight the humans are dreaming humans in their human dreams.

In innocence I died because I dared
Attempt to horizontalize the overwhelming figure 8.

Cousin Swift, you were too much poet for gloves,
But those bog-fuel were just too green to elevate

To the cherry furnace of your sacramental hate.
Only a man can make a watch; only a man can laugh.

I should prefer to hate whoever you are. However, there is room
For all of you in the outpost garrison of my dislike.

That one hundred quintars equal but a single lek is an emergency.
The humans sleep and dream elephants with anthropoid faces.

The humans awaken and grave human faces into the clouds.
Unless ingested, my mirror-shard sculptures are harmless.

They are where they are only
Because all other things are not.

Their sharp edges will not carve your surface. You won't bleed.
Should you, as they go by you, glimpse yourself,

It is you who notice you, not me.
Is the lie of the wood on the lathe or in the tree,

In hazard or in the talons of the calipers,
Or neither — but, then, perhaps in the spaces

Between the chips holding and holding the air in strangle.
I am breathing on the mirror-pane to obscure

All but your total impression of me.
Your unconscious cagescape of meridians and parallels.

Following split of the proton, the great secondary
And tertiary minds will arrive to hyena the autistica.

How to bear not being
First to the aesthetic kill.

When you find yourself masked, lashed static to a pole,
Killing-squad marching toward your dim auditory light,

Just before the storm of lead begins,
Concentrate upon until you become the word *galena*.

On this fulvus sand, my only funiculus
Between rain-forest and sea is

The spook whose shape is pellet when it isn't wave.
There is a Blick *of light between time and the elsewhen.*

I am hiding from time in the low-moving fauna of space.
I am hiding from space in the eviscerated warehouses of time.

You confuse the total eclipse of conscience
With a night without darkness.

Never has there been greater variance between
Memory of the marsupial and precisely what I've seen.

If there were anything at all anyone could do about anything,
He could pierce it with verbal inoculum and stake immediate claim.

Ye shall not pronounce me correct or wrong.
Gods have impersonated me all along.

Knowing vision of the artificial is but a dimension of the natural
Is the difference between intelligence and wisdom.

Earth was no lubricious ball to begin with. The humans
Had only to poison oases, oceans, and, of course, their own wells.

Then: to confront ideas with the open faces of curiosity.
Now: to stalk them like thieves in dark doorways and shadow.

Then: I knew. Flawlessly.
Now: The buck and blast of time. I no more know.

I wait, I memorize the habits of time, I keep faith the miscreant
Will just once return to this loculus of the crime.

The advertisements we venerate much more than others:
Stations of the cross, national flags, "Guernica".

Avoid the interior coastlines: thought staggering in rags and reeking,
Fish strangled, loaves turned to sog and mould, wine putrid,

Containers which no more contain,
And enraged bootprints, much too definitive, entirely too mooned.

Humans gift their humans with such *Gift*. For a few,
Extermination of humans is routine beside

Murder of the unwordable with arrest. Like piranhas,
Forms feed on their own in the absence of energy.

It is said they live longer in mountainous places.
I discipline myself to sleep more slowly.

The sleep which visits so elderly,
An even unevenness which trains us so softly, patiently

To wake up never. Time is moving. Or I am. Compass overload.
Gods assist us if synthesis of the syllogism, man, is only man.

There are no poems, only forms which, like guilty barristers
Speak and gesture apologetically in their stead at great cost.

Peter, from the outset, might as well have been
No fisher of fish, but a fisher of men.

The fish would have lapsed in any case. He hooked the West entire,
And it was novel to have choice between two obituaries.

If all water will not thicken and close, it might be used
Against the fire-promise. Thus the body, so the gulf.

It will be done. An expansive sigh will ease out
Through our galactic nothing and drying light.

I am a quinquevalent poison. It is forbidden to speak my name.
Should you happen upon it look to the razor clams at low tide.

Never confide to me who I am;
It'll do you boogie on my pentagram.

The tide was lower, higher when I passed this point not long ago.
I was sure I would remember. I'm here. I do not know.

I think the shadows oblique the other way.
The rocks are more or less the same.

Unless their shadows too have overturned.
Time might be easier in dense mist. Or rain.

I seem to consent it matters that things
Matter when they, almost perfectly, don't.

I am not a suicide, but a genocide;
At peril of my life, never mistake one for the other.

Infusion. Infusoria. Diaspora.
The human = the practical = the normal = the sane.

It is customary for the vanquished to surrender
His most formal weapon. In this instance: time.

Unusually, when a vessel wearies under,
A bubble-stream bursts at the surface infinitely.

More often there is no trace whatsoever
To signify that here a ship once sailed.

Lost in the fog, island summons mainland.
Imaginal unto mortal, cowhorn calls, calfhorn answers,

An evolute sound which will finally involute
From indefinite compass and blind passage

So close within the never-visible.
A horn speaks and has nothing with which to hear.

Under the water island and mainland are one.
Island persists as island to all who believe what they see.

Peaks of sunken ranges skewer
The cyanotic skin of the so-named real.

Regardless how I cordon off the past, I've been
Spotted by the opalescent eye of the peacock's tail.

At some point, any two opposing
Become interchangeable.

A troika of lightning on the west horizon. An idea
Has blundered into form too early or too late.

In this place of concrete snakes, I
With my mind for muskeg trail and jagged canyon.

I leave Anthropos in a corner fooling with his centricity
To look for the one once serious about the whales.

It is natural we measure out time by the war.
Nothing comes more organic than destruction.

When last did you register that men draw a trigger
And tease a child beneath the chin with exactly the same finger?

To declare a definite enemy
Would be to dignify one of my own kind.

I invoke the supreme doing to overcome the glacial laziness of fate.
Bad, bad minutes are swarming in the lungs of a westerly.

The coarseness of young mountains
Is not the coarseness of young cities.

In the utterly adjectival dark,
The beacon burns about a center

Which is not everywhere and casts
A circumference which is not nowhere at all.

Whatever buzzed at old skull's back door
Didn't pause while I warped remembrance even more.

To walk away an unwieldy emptiness, walk it
And walk it to the border between empty and vacuous . . .

A vacuum is armed with devast potential.
The overwhelming merely of empty is neutral

When you turn your fowling-piece toward the mint evening sky,
You will lay to waste two birds:

The gyrator who soars, sings, falls
Before a smoky stream of altogether unnatural wing,

And the one which continues to fly.
Orchis of the consciousness, as the arcane absences suade,

Always the number of dromes is greater
Than the number of abaxial competitors.

The players play at escape from their courses.
The race will go on: hope is customary.

Against the silent bulwarks of sentiment subsuming form,
Art and science are without weaponry.

For those who bend from time toward gods,
Grace will provide. Suicide. A savage satiety.

The moonfish of madness is an ordering principle.
Nationality, the tyranny of geography,

Like a uniform passed down child to child, orders and orders.
War is the order of nation in sum as in part.

Time supremely countermands. Because always almost gone,
Time is sufficient exegesis for anything.

Because I shall never exhale this breath again,
You cross my way in incalculable jeopardy,

If art imitated nature,
Indifference would become perfection.

For the sake of continuance, always must I assume I win.
Because of my accuracy . . . Or errors of my invisible adversary.

The hours empty of event, like pockets turned outside-in.
Hours, flameless, smoke a plume shape over the cinderscape.

The hours which bleed iridescence down the slopes of the dark.
The hours which spume thunder-eggs; inside them crystal forms begin.

The hours that molt new islands
To which the artificial insect will flail.

The hours shattering into the eyes of the snowcaps about them,
These hours which destroy themselves so gladly,

Only the warm pit remains, hardening angles of evidence,
And memory of yellow upon the weary air.

These hypocycloid parades we name wars have been
Small routine manoeuvres. The war is on its way.

Never did a single beast slouch toward a single destination
The ammoniac reek of terrified animal was everywhere.

There is, as yet, no remedy for the common death. Conceal yourself.
Conserve your heat. Keep the faith with time.

Time by time, space by space,
Cell by cell, form by form, nothing by nothing,

Beyond intuition, beyond cognition,
Beyond the final rage of human cage and container,

The approach of it inexorable:
From a disorder of time different from this,

A space strange to us perfectly,
Perhaps a no/time-no/space,

But in motion, without question, countergrowth
Toward these coordinates, toward this chronology,

In transport by means not of this knowledge.
Men say they have somewhat to do with it.

Women feel they have it in the flesh encaged.
Radial, perhaps, to a disfamiliar axis,

Its nourishment at conception arrests
And, therefore, is not evident at the doorway:

Knowledge of a wholly other duration
Gone dormant as a garden viper in December

In the north of a northern country
For the long, cold circumference of longevity.

Occasionally, foreign stirrings far away
In a Tasmanian thicket of the head

Give suspicion of a difference
Between the dormant and the dead.

Loose the creatures from my figures
To carry me away. Edges of the edges are caving.

Time returns to return to where all the clear streams start,
But there's not enough left now to reach those high crags of the heart.

Beyond the last trees, the meadows are greener than any green
Of sea. And I'll never scale again to that height of me.

The space I do not occupy narrows as the time grinds short.
I decide this has been a calling, profession, or a sport.

I squander energy never mine to make form come when it can,
And all the time I don't believe to sustain the maker, not the man.

A part of me is hidden in every shadow of your rooms.
I'm a swarm of dark words sometimes in the plague of shape,

Sometimes in the shape of a dog with only three legs.
Water requires organization. The Babel inflorescence

Has nothing whatsoever to do with language.
To claim understanding formally is to issue invitation to war.

Declare your emptiness at customs.
Only the empty can be used.

Better words wear the stench of fish
Than grow rich in the odor of rodent.

The things of darkness are darkness
Except for a photon cone dying down.

A beam turning gives substance only in intermittance,
In almost unmeaning serial, like peaks and reefs

Just beneath the surfaces of light.
The lighthouse to the automatic craft:

You will founder, come near me, you will sink.
Ship to light: Burn on and on and on and out:

All who dare incandesce
Must immensely die.

The mechanics, mirages and mirrors of my lighthouse —
There have been so many, many ends of the worlds.

There are far fewer lighthouses than ships
And many more dangers than both in sum.

The numbers come equivalent
At the final undertug of sun.

Light is always at once in at least two places.
Not the large seasons. The small ones. Between.

Small bars at the river-mouth,
Small aid across wide moving water,

The tide turns and turns again
And one returns wet with not returning.

Sudden the shock of cold water in a boot
Half-way across a stream which seemed so shallow.

Shalom, Azazel, *splendid demon:*
The serpent was such a crude wood-wind,

A fair thought for coarse cause, and low, low register tone.
My back and forth and back and forth

Is high-slack, low-slack of the tide,
And when the unwending pivot comes,

I prefer it had been an indifferent ride.
Space the time, time the rhythm, and light the inaudible melody,

Darkness was the silence he listened to,
The mountain man gone down to sea.

———